This Peculiarly Peaceful Light

This Peculiarly Peaceful Light

Poems by

Ron Roth

© 2023 Ron Roth. All rights reserved.
This material may not be reproduced in any form, published,
reprinted, recorded, performed, broadcast,
rewritten or redistributed without
the explicit permission of Ron Roth.
All such actions are strictly prohibited by law.

Cover design by Shay Culligan
Cover image and author's photo by Ron Roth

ISBN: 978-1-63980-346-0

Kelsay Books
502 South 1040 East, A-119
American Fork, Utah 84003
Kelsaybooks.com

For Pat, always.

Acknowledgments

My sincere thanks to Kelsay Books for publishing this collection. I am especially thankful for my wife Pat, who is not only the inspiration for many of these poems but also provided feedback and advice. Paul Gillies, old friend and fellow poet, continues to encourage me and share his own distinctive voice as a poet.

Contents

This Quilt Called Memory

Weeping Tree	17
Downstream	19
Sestina: I Harvest This Quilt Called Memory	20
Perfect Pitch	22
The Playground	23
Roadmaster	25
The Pier	26
January 1957	27
Night Ships	28
Beloved	29
Old Friends	30

This Peculiarly Peaceful Light

Psalm	33
This Peculiarly Peaceful Light	35
May River	36
The Sound	37
The Burning Bush	38
There's a Mockingbird Outside	39
The Pretender	41
Ballerina	42
Orchard	43
Sunset	44

Our Groove

Our Groove	47
The Straw Fedora	48
Holy Land	49
The Waiting Room	51
Come with Me Now	52
Even When the Leaves Are Still	53

What I Miss Most

What I Miss Most	57
Van Gogh's *Avenue of the Poplars*	59
Rembrandt's *Return of the Prodigal Son*	60
The French Poplars	61
The Bittersweet Hour	62
Rembrandt's *The Teacher*	63
For W. A.	64

Here Is Our Family

Here Is Our Family: Pandemic	67
The Blessing of the Animals	69
Lucy	71
The Bicyclist	72
Elegy: The Ukraine	74
Flossenberg	76
Morocco	78
A Playlist for My Passing	81

And even when the long twilight and the weariness of death come,
you will not set in our sky, you advocate of life.
New stars you have let us see, and new wonders of the night.

—Friedrich Nietzsche

This Quilt Called Memory

Weeping Tree

Toward the river,
outside the church's window,
a weeping tree.
Its limbs fall
in a melancholy
fountain bending downward
in cascade,
pacific rhythms.
A squirrel climbs
inside its shelter,
snooping in an inquisitive way
for fugitive berries
the birds have overlooked.

In the pew I see the wrinkles
on my hands, crinkling—
dry, parched,
leaving tracks
like those you see on Mars,
my body's tentative steps
toward dust, heading for
another universe
with splendid views of nebulae,
the immortal stars.

Emperor Aurelius observed
the closing of a life is not the end,
but transformation,
our dust will enter flowers,
the breath of someone's prayer
a thousand years away,
the spruce of a violin yet to be made,
played by someone yet to be born,

under a grove of bent trees
yet to be grown;
a lone and loony 12-year-old,
making cartwheels through the sea bream
on a beach somewhere
in a tide yet to come in.

Downstream

The Romans had a custom,
lined hallways in their homes
with marble sculptures,
alabaster busts of ancestors
revered for certain virtues:
a bent toward timely humor,
a steadiness of purpose.

Like a Roman, I do my duty:
place memorial flowers behind the church's
altar for my oldest friend;
a park bench in an arboretum
in memory of an aunt,
a brass plaque with her name;
the gold ring I wear, my mother's,
its lion's head set with diamonds in its eyes,
I kiss it now and then.

Who will honor me,
far downstream in time,
after my ashes have been
scattered on the Sound?

Perhaps my grandson,
casting a line into the Niobrara,
and as it arcs upward
over the river a flash of memory,
an image: me standing over him
in a gurney in the hospital ER.
Just us.
My voice whispering
like the murmur of that river,
"I am here, I'm here."

Sestina: I Harvest This Quilt Called Memory

I harvest this quilt called memory,
made of coarse spun material layered under silk
and in each square a face,
living quietly in its landscape,
vague, pleasant portraits torn
from the moorings of their moment, again and again

they tell their stories, again and again,
singing in their islands of memory,
their words fluttering like torn,
banners of silk
flying over a landscape
sculpted in vague contours of the past, its face.

How would I describe that face?
Changing with each season, again and again
I expectantly search for each landscape,
the balm of its ancient memory,
a soothing ointment, a raiment of silk,
healing my spirit, halting and torn.

Many times has it been torn,
shorn of all beauty, its face
riven in discolor, a perverted jockey's silk,
reminding me again and again
that nothing is sure, even memory
can be lost against this landscape.

Now old age inhabits the landscape,
—but gladly—unlike Lear, torn
and tormented by the past, by memory,
the barren stare in his face
reliving sad tales again and again,
the membrane against madness sheer as silk.

My good fortune is to have this quilt, its silk
surface comforting, covering my past's landscape
with grace, reliving again and again
moods, warm and friendly feelings not torn
away and missing, but present now, a face
smiling through time, through memory.

The silk is worn, its torn fragments
litter the landscape, embroidering a face:
again and again, the golden memory, the sacred space.

Perfect Pitch

Fifty years ago, an F sharp sung
from a pitch pipe,
found its way into the voices
of men in a farmhouse parlor
just north of Pittsburgh,
away from the mills,
air cleaned by the chafe of the wind.

Outside the window
light faded and twitched between the trees,
the view gave nothing back.
In the parlor, its walls
covered with old photographs,
ancestors looked on
while hymn notes rose like flowers,
from a steel worker,
a bus driver,
a salesman
and a carpenter,
bringing the men closer
to the promised land, its perfect pitch,
in the garden "Where the dew is still on the roses."

The Playground

There,
trilling under a palm tree's spikey dome,
somewhere in the marsh,
stately, stalking,
picking at some shells,
a heron.

The sun's eye widens in the east,
splintering some vagrant clouds,
light shafts sweeping the tidal flow
into the sea, into its azure layers.

I'm taking it all in,
following a path,
a back road out of the dingy sadness
laying across the day.

I plunge into memory,
yearning for a moment
in the gleeful arc
of a playground swing,
legs thrust straight out
vaulting me upward into
momentary, eyes-closed
weightlessness, brisk, sweet letting go,
the free-wheeling whisk
of the body, taut, straining
for one more flight
higher by just an inch.
I climb up the ladder of a slide,
riding it down on a sled of wax paper,
the split second of propulsion
exploding off the lip at the bottom,

deftly landing on the feet
and into a run,
the toss of my smiling head.

Roadmaster

Summer's lush language
spoke to me then
racing through the tall grasses
on my sleek, red Roadmaster,
its silver fenders and white sidewalls
speeding past the "Pop Stand"
with its penny candy, comic books
and quaint oak post office
where I checked for word from my "steady."

I set shuffleboard lanes
with their cues and discs
under the wooden shelter,
its deep matted spiders' webs
dank with age, swept clear by the breezes
gusting off Lake Erie
while I kept a watchful eye
for flying saucers rising from its dark heart.

The old-time tabernacle with its stiff, hard pews
rang with our hymns
before the altar where my sisters
sang their duets, and Mr. Fussner,
the organ impresario,
played riffs on *What a Friend,*
while the sun pulled
me into the lazy, beguiling days.

The Pier

The pier,
off the beach to the west,
was built by army engineers:
huge blocks of sandstone,
a ton each, like the pharaohs made,
strewn abreast
the river's slim channel,
the Vermilion.

My first romance was consummated
on a beach towel on those stones,
its architecture's anonymity perfect
for our crazed pleasures,
breathlessly played out to the rhythm
of the waves, lapping against the stones.

Mornings a creaking fleet
of fishing boats lumbered furtively
out of the river's mouth on the prowl for perch.
At dusk the parade returned guided
by the pier's blinking lights.
Further west the lights
of Cedar Point and Marblehead
flickered at the edge of the world.

The pier's red beacon winked,
faint in the eye of the fading, orange sun
settling into the lake,
while an audience on the beach
on cheap folding chairs
applauded and cheered.

January 1957

Our Lake Erie, frozen over,
deeply quiet against our breaths
hanging in the air in puffs.
The shore strewn with ice baskets,
giant crystals sheering the pale sun's
light into shards,
glowing with an inner light,
twinkling at the edges.
We stepped carefully over the surface,
its stark white plain,
the fine grains of sand that sifted through
our toes in summer now locked away.

A drone flies over the lake,
I patch it in.
It hovers over
the gaunt, giant stillness,
its frigid, sullen stare.
The ice jams and fractures the shore
where one summer night we saw
Sputnik sputtering across the sky,
there, where the edge of the lake curves
along the beach like a smile.

Night Ships

I listened to them through the cheap earpiece
of a plastic toy I ordered from a cereal box.
Clipped it to the metal bed frame
to make it work, heard faint signals,
the chatter of sea captains,
on their huge ships,
conversations between old salts, loners,
somewhere in the lake's vast solitude,
in the perfection of its silence.
The dim shape of the ships glided
through the night, leaving crystalline wakes,
lustrous in the meager light.
I imagined their lights,
flickering distantly, ethereally.

Beloved

My conception was the stuff of dreams.

My birth parents met at the movies
in Weirton, West Virginia.
The Strand, back in the day
when a theater was a temple
with long, plush curtains, royal blue,
blanketing the stage and silver sconces
sparkling on the walls.

Was my father an usher in a smart red jacket
garnished with gold buttons? My mother
a cigarette girl walking the lobby
with a tray of Lucky Strikes and Camels
in a pert short skirt and sheer dark nylons?

They shared a secret room
while I grew inside of her.
He never left her side,
saw to it I'd find my way
to a woman who could not bear her own
and a father who lifted me up
like a gift from God.

What miraculous luck, mine.
Parents on both sides of birth
who loved me well,
not by design.

Old Friends

T'is a gift
I've rediscovered them,
remembering dreams of deeds
that we would do
in the gleaming prospect of this world,
ready to roar into life's first act
guileless, shorn of every
shoddy time the years would bring.

We laid on blankets listening
to a concert on the "Point"
where three rivers met,
the music rising sweetly from a barge
that rested grandly on the river,
night receiving it so gladly
we thought its beauty would
follow us forever,
into days and nights,
everything to come,
as we went our ways
and disappeared.

Then, on the other side of decades,
they reappeared,
their signals weak but still broadcasting,
making way through
evenings long with memories,
embers casting golden glow,
sweetly, sweetly,
on the narrowing road.

This Peculiarly Peaceful Light

Psalm

I lift my eyes to the scattering clouds,
stunned by the sun's white fire,
sculpted by winds
into inexhaustible tableaux
moving across blue plains.

Sacred the hawks, the swallow-tailed ones
looping below the clouds,
thrusting upward exuberant in tailwinds,
and the warblers below,
flitting from branch to branch,
their bracing enthusiasm;
and the mourning doves
loping with regal aplomb through emerald
sheaves of grass.

Blessed the sea,
the oracular sea,
its depths filled with miraculous beings
its surface surging
with the waves' great swells,
their sage rhythms, their gravitas.

Holy the river,
quiet pilgrim,
weaving through the land,
current flowing
with the sureness of a great soul.
Grebes and mergansers slip down
its terraced banks into solitude
and over them hang the ancient limbs
of live oaks and cottonwoods,
old, stooped men, contemplating.

Bless the morning
shrouds of mist hovering over
its calm waters,
and evening's final sounds
echoing down its flume,
glancing off its surface
into night's sweet loom.

This Peculiarly Peaceful Light

The clouds,
great, billowing herds of them
stride epically through the sky
with their grand gestures,
over the sheer, still waters
of the Chicheesee River,
its current just visible
in the slim branches
drifting on its surface.

From the nearby bridge,
the glum drone of traffic,
its concrete buttresses
cast long shadows over
the dead still marsh grass.
An eagle circles pensively
in inscrutable rhythms
over my meditation
sitting on a picnic table,
near the old, wooden pier.
The place from which one day
my ashes will flow easily
toward the ocean,
scoured clean of vanity,
flowing into the immense,
mystery of the Sound,
while on their regal wings
some pelicans see me through the passage
into the peculiarly peaceful light.

May River

The live oaks
bower the road along the river
with their wreaths of weary limbs,
creaking in the stiff winds climbing the bluffs,
trellised with silvery showers of spanish moss
cascading down and over the portal
with the soft patina of an old engraving.

At the end of the road
the board and battened chapel overlooks
the pluff-mud flats ringed by reefs of oyster beds.
Over the swales of marshes a bad-ass osprey
jets across the treetops with a red fish
in its talons, headfirst above the long shafts
of loblolly pines.

Follow the river to the ocean and the beaches
sculpted by the whims of winds, where marooned
red mangrove bushes and their spiky branches
jumble in delirious patterns. Dense stands
of panic grass spring from the sand in green fountains,
and maiden cane, its stems tipped by thin bristles.

Further back the marshes,
wander among the meadows,
oyster catchers in their iridescent coats,
stalk with inquisitive aplomb.
Near the shore
a piping plover and its twiggy legs
high-steps through the glistening rills of sand,
drenched in the tidal flow,
in repeating rhythms,
like musical notations.

The Sound

A flounder lays in shallows,
its pale tan oval invisible,
blended in the sand.
Nearby a hermit crab
dolefully drags its shell,
passing by a blue one,
resting in profound complacency.

The wind moves over the rivers,
sculpting them with ripples,
echoing, supple patterns.
Under the pier the tide
flows out to Port Royal Sound,
its vast haven surging with life:
the oyster beds, temples
harboring great civilizations,
the lampreys gliding through
headwaters with suave, balletic ease;
jellyfish billowing,
rising slo-mo in their pink-fringed clouds,
water-bound nebulae
forming in the Sound's universe.
Then finally out to the sea,
the grave, majestic sea,
where the unanswered questions
seem irrelevant,
caught up as they are
in the sure, flow of the tides.

The Burning Bush

Autumn
and our backyard's lone crepe myrtle's
blooms turn quickly into flame,
a pyre of flagrant, pulsing pinks,
upsetting summer's sylvan calm,
holding court, proud monarch,
over its backyard dominion.

Urgently sparrows
fly into it, then out.
What does it mean,
this burning bush?

Its leaves, battered and pocked,
glow in their final
brilliant statements.
A parting,
as the wind sweeps them
into the woods, scuffling over
the patio stones,
their sound like muffled applause,
an orderly retreat
into winter's solace.

There's a Mockingbird Outside

There's a mockingbird outside
the window, before first light,
chirping in hard, urgent voice
without music or finesse,
flying off to leave some droppings
on my Honda's rear view mirror.

Scamp!

In Charleston
I followed a mischief-maker
down Calhoun Street
while walking to the clinic.
There, perched on top a honey locust tree
that's scratching out a life
in the concrete and the fumes,
he trilled tunes, arias,
thrilling in their sweetness.

I cannot believe birds live
oblivious to joy.
Think of those undulating
clouds of them, their synchronous
swales that seem as one, euphoric mind.

In the backyard bluebirds fly giddily
to the feeder while cardinals chase
each other through bushes,
bursting out of them toward
the treetops like jets in a dog fight
strafing the ground with guano.

Ancient Peruvians
made clay pots decorated
with images of owls, pelicans, and parrots,
likenesses cloaked
in whimsical designs,
in raiments of earth-bound colors,
bold umbers, reds, and yellows.
Sacred objects of the everyday,
they depicted them with familial respect,
their unassuming magic,
their divine connection.

The Pretender

Such a contrarian, this camelia bush.
Its magenta petals
not the regal red of roses,
nor the lilies' chaste elegance,
just in your face cheerful,
its golden stamens
poking the frigid morning good naturedly.
It powers up its deep green leaves,
its winter suit dappled with gay boutonnieres.
It entertains some cardinals,
flitting about its boughs.
It wobbles in the wind
like its had a few too many,
pretending to be a Christmas tree.

Ballerina

That quirky flight of butterflies
bobbing, weaving in the shape
of a happily unhinged mind:
blithe ballerinas of the backyard.
Prancing to the siren scent of nectar,
subject to the whims of wind,
riding it like surfers,
then back to business,
aloof yet curious.
Like the time one landed
for a moment on a wave
of my wife's hair,
coaxing a smile
out of the tight, prim
lips of morning.

Orchard

A bronzed sheen reflecting
off the tree trunks,
glows through the forest
with the warmth
of ripened peaches
stacked in braided baskets
in a roadside stand,
harvested from an orchard
plaited in perfect symmetry,
where in the evening shadows
glide slowly over the land,
laying it to rest in deep quietness,
in the consoling, lingering light.

Sunset

There's a piety
I reserve for sunset,
the stillness it requires,
the resonance it applies to memory;
its deft, sifting through time
to find a moment I had neglected,
as the sun recedes from sight,
indifferent in its beauty,
and seagulls clap their wings
for yet another brave performance.

Our Groove

Our Groove

What was their name, that band
that rocked from a bare stage
on an empty, Nebraska field,
where we swayed freely
back and forth like the blue stems
on those once vast plains?

They played between
their big, black amps
that blared the music
over the hills' soft swales,
over indifferent cows
in the shallows on the Platte.

The brash brunette,
perched on
sparkling, red high heels,
belting out the words into the night,
into our young, lithe limbs,
our arms weaving their way
around each other's waists,
in the luxuriant grip
of the moment's self-forgetting.

You insisted that we dance, and we did:
in backroom bars,
in living rooms
and under stars.

We'll always find a dance floor somewhere.
A jukebox somewhere waits
for our spins and twirls, our songs,
our "just ours" special groove,
our sweet embrace.

The Straw Fedora

There I am, in my straw fedora,
you sitting in front of me,
on that shaky folding chair
we found miraculously waiting for us
along that elm lined road
with the Louvre behind us
shrouded in a mist,
me leaning over your shoulder
all rakish and movie star cool.

Later, holding it at my side,
I peer out the second floor window
of a left bank café
framed in shadow,
a picture of light pastels,
an ochre rooftop floating
in the midday sun
above a green-framed window
where a cat muses on its ledge.

Later still, the hat's brim flapping
in the wind, bicycling down the road
to Monet's lily pads at Giverny,
chiming the bike's bell wildly,
I stop and rest in a chapel along the way,
place the hat on a cane-seated chair
where it lays in light, the light
of stained-glass windows.

Holy Land

On a morning with the cool air
lying on the land
we walked the field they say
the shepherds heard the angels
and their "good tidings."
We heard the priests' words echo
through the cypress on the Mount of Olives.
No miracles on our journey, no water into wine,
but the faithful's chants glancing off the walls
of chapels celebrating Mass.

Under the shadow of barbed wire
we saw pilgrims, their white robes
billowing like clouds around them
as they sank into the river Jordan
for their baptisms. At its edge we knelt,
filling bottles with its waters.

Past dusk, in the Negev Desert
near Abraham's well, our headlights spot
some Bedouins, wanderers.
They greet us hawking souvenirs,
then turn and kneel toward Mecca
on their prayer rugs.
They have no camels, just a donkey
following us vacantly up a rocky trail,
to a view of the Valley of Death,
filled with the effluvia of time
flowing glacially downward
though the darkening swales of sand.
Above, the sweep of steel-white stars
flowed with the rhythm of the dunes,
each in their purity, their nakedness,
indifferent in their glory.

On the west shore of the Sea of Galilee
Mary Magdalene's memory lingers
in her small hometown, Magdala.
She knew Magdala's synagogue
where a spare stone bench remains
from which Christ might have taught.

We held hands and walked among the ruins,
a maze of ancient homes' foundations.
If I had lost my faith
you helped me gather some of its remains,
like shards of shattered pots of clay
strewn among the site. Perhaps we could
reassemble some of what remained,
like the recently revealed mosaic that we saw,
next to a crumbling hearth,
its colors vivid still, after all that time.

The Waiting Room

How could I have known
the bleak beauty of this waiting room
without your patient hand in mine
transmitting that faint signal, hope.
We're happy with this
less appreciated form of love: devotion.
It tenderly reminds me
that were I lost you'd find
my arm and walk me
to a grove and with your
sweet perfume
refresh my memory.
Finding you I'd take you
to our backyard,
hold you in my arms,
and watch the darting chickadees,
the glittering buntings
in evening's quiet light.

Come with Me Now

Come with me now and pass pleasant hours.
This day and its charms, then night's twinkling stars,
will take us away, will be our own flowers.

The years now have left us blessed with some powers
to savor the moment and not waste the time,
so come with me now and pass pleasant hours.

The dogwood's pink petals, spring's gentle showers,
are there for the taking, fair and sublime,
with night's twinkling stars, our very own flowers.

Though time is now fleeting we still have our powers
to admire magnolias, their grace, their design,
so come with me now and pass pleasant hours.

No one will know, our secret bowers,
the places we share our love's sweet rhyme,
and hold in our hands, our own lovely flowers.

Now and forever these places are ours
where our private joys will have their own time.
So come with me now and pass pleasant hours,
with the night's fairest stars, our very own flowers.

Even When the Leaves Are Still

Even when the leaves are still
the song-birds silent
and sunset's colors fade,
I will love you.

And when the hymns
we sang in the old church on the river
where we held each other's hands
are silent
I will love you then.

And when eternity opens up its arms
and time no longer matters,
and we shelter in its care
I will love you.

And when you wake
and walk among the stars
I will follow you
and will be yours forever
and will love you,
always love you,
I will love you.

What I Miss Most

What I Miss Most

What I miss most is museums,
their galleries' calming flow,
their labels' steadying certainty,
as I contemplate Van Gogh;
the many bins of magnets
arrayed throughout their stores,
masterworks I will include,
to curate an exhibit
on my refrigerator's door.

There's an emerald garden, a Daubigny,
that I adore on bended knee.
Now "Show me the Monet!",
a lily pad or two,
their little loads of stacked up paint,
trembling in the dew.

I'll take my morning latte
with a little, creamy dollop,
like the restless random drippings
of a fearsome Jackson Pollack.

Here is Fra Angelica,
his best Annunciation,
with a cherub and a putti,
dancing on a little cloud
in happy celebration.

I miss the mists of Venice,
the palace of the doges,
with Tintoretto's murals,
depicting them at Mary's feet
in supplicating poses.

So until the world no longer reels,
the virus lost its sway,
when museums' doors are opened wide
and we all come out and play,
I'll sit around and bide my time
perusing first editions,
until the time I can cast my eye
on the wondrous glow of Titian.

Van Gogh's *Avenue of the Poplars*

Where did he see that light,
that affectionate light of autumn, of vespers?
Brash red plumes rise from the poplars
on their slim stilts,
under summer's dome,
its deep blue delaying
interment in the winter's crypt.

Amber burnished fence posts
stooped in age cast enigmatic shadows,
remnants of a perfect life.
The trees, a cathedral's spacious walls,
cover the road like a nave,
sheltering a nun in her pensive habit,
walking through the shadows,
through melancholic pools of orange,
summer's darkening embers.
Birds chatter in the treetops,
their voices a choir.

Rembrandt's *Return of the Prodigal Son*

Love never traced an easy path for us.
Its rare appearance came after long
seasons of scorched earth,
holding each other, weeping.

The portion I left for you,
awkward, formal, correct,
was seldom the pure fountain
of that embrace, the leap
of my prodigal heart,
clothed in my brown, threadbare raiment
after my wandering in the wilderness.

I caught a glimpse of your face
as you waved goodbye,
my last view of you,
like the father in the Prodigal Son:
tender, plaintive,
content.

The French Poplars

—After a painting by Willie Betty Newman

If ever there was color
with a kind embrace
it is this pale violet
glowing through the poplar trees.
It empties
into dusk's quiet breath,
suspended in the summer's
fleeing green plush.
Eyes closed,
I lean backward,
into its luster,
the tall trees falling
back against the world.
their leaves fading in shadows,
in stillness.

The Bittersweet Hour

10:00 pm.
Driving off the island,
my head singing with Sibelius.
I see a quick store parking lot
radiating cool gray light,
Hopper's light,
his brittle palette.
I see the empty stares
of his people, the nighthawks.
The lengthening shadows,
crepe draperies;
longing's spare offering,
the bittersweet hour.

Rembrandt's *The Teacher*

In his studio,
its southern, facing side,
late afternoon,
the hour when quiet light
seeks shelter in the earth's old soul,
he lays down an amber ground,
tempering it with varnishes,
layered glazes rising to the surface
with an inner glow,
tinting the canvas weave
in a wash of dreaminess.

In the scuffling path of his brush
a faint, gold halo rests above
the teacher's brow,
the oracular hollows of his eyes
wide with refined resignation,
darkened suns setting
over his long wanderings,
the light's weak radiance
passing over him,
the consoling earth,
ready to receive him.

For W. A.

In Stockholm at an art museum
I viewed a sculpture of you as a child
contemplating a violin half your size.
I paused, remembered,
when my father died,
your *Requiem* gave me solace,
music melding pathos and tranquility,
expressing feelings,
some I could not name.
I listened in a trance of recognition,
surprised at what you knew,
followed you trustingly into my grief,
met that lovely youth
who extinguishes the flame
and calms the billowing sea.

Here Is Our Family

Here Is Our Family: Pandemic

The father watching his daughter
stretched out and still, in unrequited sleep,
her heart, its moth-light beat fading.

The wife, her shaking hands,
doing her best at a prayer for her,
slipping away
under the hood of a plastic mask
without the touch of a hand.

The sister who sang in the mornings
in bed with her spaniel,
now lost and silent in an unmarked grave
with a hundred other silent sleepers.

The homeless man stretched
out and laying on a suite
of subway seats at midnight
on the J Train rumbling through
the tunnels, their ebony oblivion
his final resting place,
covered by a dirty painter's drop,
his shroud, his body bag.

The boy,
propped on his father's shoulder
waving to his Nana
behind a barrier of glass,
laying in a wasteland strewn
with wheezing metal boxes
trapped in a cocoon
of rubber tubes and wires
like snake coils, smothering her,
contesting every breath.

She requested music in her room,
a hymn, *Cristo, Yo Te Amo*.
(She hears faint strains of tango
from the dance floor
of a club in Queens.)

Her sister leads a midnight vigil,
prayers for her. A nurse has laid
a prayer card for her on her pillow:
Christ's outstretched arms
against the outline of a tree,
the tree of life,
its sagging boughs
give shelter to a lamb.

The Blessing of the Animals

The sun gilds the river with golden strands
as the tide flows in wandering into the arms
of the emerald shore stirring with barks
and chirps. The faithful and their dogs,
cats and canaries are queuing up
in front of the old church on the river.
Like the ark, it gathers them in.

Inside its peach-colored walls, a priest prepares
the holy water, blessing it in the arc of his arm,
then enters the yard, grand in his holy vestments.
There's an old, stooped couple,
led by their perky Pomeranian.
A woman carries a cage with her parrot,
chattering in its many-colored coat.
There's a hamster, encircled by a young family.
And is that a goat near the end of the line?

We hold our Lucy, old girl.
She passes out her blessings,
licking the hand of a woman
in the nearby park:
"Our dog of thirteen years
just passed on,"
she says, crying softly.

We trust them in the space
of our most secret lives,
with our confessions,
our tales of disappointment.
St. Francis understood
the load they carried for us.

Looking out upon the river,
there's a widow with her spaniel
cradled in her arms,
like a woman on Nantucket
centuries ago, waiting for her husband
lost at sea.

Lucy

A dry wind weaves the boughs
at forest's edge.
They sway languidly
pulsing in the rhythm
of a flagging heart,
in the clearing where
we laid white petals
in a garland for you.

Leaves rustle in indifference
through our bleak ceremony
as we remember you running
over the broad, green
hills of Pennsylvania.

Our eyes rise to the treetops
for signs of your soul
rising through the dim shade
of branches while leaves murmur.
As the wind dies the boughs droop
in the forest's calm,
our love suspended
in grief's spaciousness.
Sleep gently,
sleep peacefully now.

The Bicyclist

As I fumbled with the air pump
an old man, gaunt and lean
like John Lee Hooker
ambled over from his bicycle
laying on the parking lot curb.
I've seen these men on their bicycles
hugging the edge of the road,
threading the white paint strip
like daredevils.

"Can you spare a quarter sir?"
I snap back, "Not now pal, not now."
Pouring down, the rain
soaked me as I searched
for a fugitive tire valve cap.
Walking back to his bike,
his shoulder's drooped
under a neon, orange vest.

I collapse into the car,
slam the door and rev the engine.
Pat says gently,
"Aren't you going to give him something?"
I look over the steering wheel
into the gray rain thinking,
what was it some philosopher said?
"Never resist a generous impulse."
Got out of the car
and pulled out a five,
handed it to the man.

He smiled gaily,
stunned by his good luck.
Danced back to his bike,
leaping like one of the Nicholas brothers
snapping his taps.

Elegy: The Ukraine

—for Oksana

The war grinds on,
the presence of the dead,
their pale, hollow voices,
their longing
under the jack boot
no sorrow can survive,
the calliope of howls,
shrill screams of missiles
disintegrating in the rubble
of disinterested buildings.

It never ends,
the bloody gauntlet
they must pass,
dying with no guarantee
that love will last.

Man the barricades,
pull out all the stops,
tend to every child,
that those flowers
not be lost.

Pray to that God
who seems to have disappeared,
perhaps He will return
whenever the coast is clear.

Leaves blanket the land
under the halo of an eagle's
circle of flight,
over the gray debris of battle,
a blessing on the soldiers,
the boys dying below.

Restless, the delicate wind
covers them with tenderness,
sends them into the silent sea of grass,
their slowly swaying swales,
their deep seclusion,
bearing them back into the earth.

Flossenberg

"Flossenberg, Ich weisse nicht."
I heard this many times
on my search for that Nazi killing center,
to witness a small portion of the hell
that never touched me.
Even then in '73,
hitchhiking in the south of Deutschland,
the coverup continued by those
"Good" Germans who claimed they
had never heard the name.

I met a trucker in a bar,
said he knew the way,
found the narrow path that led down
to a bowl-shaped clearing,
bounded by some concrete posts,
remnants of the electric fence.
A barren mist covered the guard tower,
in its shadow an earthen pyramid covered
with pale grass, sheltered the bones and ashes
of some 40,000 souls, their holy remains.

I stood in front of the stone execution wall,
to see the last sight of the life left
to the Jews, the gypsies,
the priests and politicians
who had perished there.
Stillness, bitter stillness
as I walked the short path to the ovens,
a rusted gurney holding a wreath
of parched, dead lilies,
a yellowed banner,
"Plus Jamais! Plus Jamais!"

Each day I receive a picture
from the Holocaust Museum,
one of the lost.

A French child, six,
his photograph in a gold, oval frame
sitting on a checkered tablecloth,
holding a stuffed animal, a lamb.
He perished in Auschwitz.

Another child, even younger,
Judith Herschle, a Hungarian Jew,
murdered in an Auschwitz gas chamber.

Another, younger still,
Eszter Abraham,
born August 1942,
laying back in a baby carriage
pushed by his mother,
killed two years later.

You who read this will know them now.
Please harbor a small haven of remembrance for them,
their immortal beauty,
the fact of their lives;
that before the catastrophe
in the embrace of life,
they knew joy
before it passed them into the night.

Morocco

1973.
My year of living adventurously.
Hitchhiking through Europe
with a backpack and pea jacket.
I'd had enough of great cathedrals,
headed south through France.
Nights in hostels, one with a cage
filled with exotic birds
where an Englishman sketched
a warbler singing on a swing.

Traveling south through Marseille's dirty streets
and seedy alleys then making fast across
the Mediterranean on a ferry
to Morocco and to Fez, the ancient city,
its medina's winding, narrow streets
unchanged these thousand years,
with the sour smell of leather being cured
in back lots, strung out and drying in the sun,
and piles of steaming olives,
their aroma mingling with sandalwood and citrus.
Copper pots, brass kettles hung from the eaves
of storefronts, their merchants constant babble,
"How much you pay for this? How much?"

I found the entrance of a mosque.
Pristine desert light glistened from its
open courtyard's floor where a solitary man
prayed, sitting cross-legged wearing a white turban.
The call to prayer broadcasts from the nearby muezzin,
a slim, round tower wired with a loudspeaker.
"Ahhhhh Lahhhh" drones across the clamor
of the city: high-pitched, tinny, yearning.

A man approached me, "Is it not beautiful?"
I nod my head. He leads me to a crumbling façade,
an ancient university's remains, once an observatory
to chart the movement of the stars.
Its open porch welcomed the light of learning
weaving through its arch's intricate carvings
like music, its fluted columns, designed
for nothing more than ravishing the eyes,
even now, as they crumble into dust.

Next day I woke to noisy streets.
Outside long snaking lines of men and women
dancing to exotic rhythms in frenzied celebration
of Mohammed's birthday. Reedy shrieks of mizmars
mingled in the air with clouds of hashish
rising from the old men pulling on their hookahs
in the casbah's dim cafes. I watched a water vendor
with his long, slim, silver carrier, its tinkling bells
and tin water cups, while women in their hijabs
and chadors spun and reveled under Allah's gaze.

One of them with laughing eyes pulled me
through the throng then to an alley
under unrelenting sun flailing every surface
with its harsh midday regime. She led me
to a parched, oak door.
Inside and sitting on the floor on cushions,
her family. Her turbaned father
raised his hand and gestured me to sit.
She took her place,
pulled off her veil revealing impish lips,
a lean face smiling with unconscious pleasure.
Bezhiza was a seamstress and she sewed
beneath a wall shelf with a television broadcasting
Perry Mason reruns in Arabic.

Her father had a sense of humor, would pull my leg.
One day he asked how many camels
I thought his daughter worth? What kind of dowry
could I provide? I paused. Was he joking?
If not, my answer might bring insult on his family.
I smoked Camels in those days, twenty to a pack.
I looked him in the eye.
"Vingt!" I said with great authority.
"Vingt!" He laughed and slapped his knee.

I wonder what became of her.
Has her face darkened with the sun,
wise with crow's feet trails embroidering
her laughing eyes? Does she still remember
our encounter, its fugitive sweetness,
those three evenings when we strolled
the streets, the breezes with their fragrant
hints of heather and valerian draining down
the nearby Atlas Mountains,
the violet clouds laying down their trails,
blanketing the remnants of the sun
receding slowly through the limbs of lemon trees.

A Playlist for My Passing

Ah! Vivaldi's *Four Seasons*.
Spring, the violins chirp like birds,
deliriously joyful ones,
their notes dancing with the cellos and bass viols below
in their steady motion.

Then Mozart, his *Ave Verum Corpus,*
looking for that perfect
final note, its exquisite yearning.
Wait for it...Wait for it...
He gathers it in,
suspends it like a star.

That note finds its way into a Bach partita.
A solo violin, great soul,
thrusts its voice higher into exultant possibilities,
shaping the image of a beautiful prayer,
the beatitude our life can be.

Then Schumann,
his tender lullabies for children.
And Ravel, his *Fairy Garden,*
Its farewell to childhood.
(Remember?
We heard it under the big tent in Aspen.)

One guilty pleasure: Erik Satie,
his insouciant nonchalance.
Light as a wisp of morning mist,
refreshing as an aperitif.

And finally, Ives,
The Unanswered Question,
its brace of woodwinds
flowing slowly like a river,
toward the veiled world.

About the Author

Ron Roth's poetry and fiction have appeared in the *South Carolina Bards* anthology, *Bellingham Review, South Dakota Review, Great River Review, The Panhandler, The McGuffin,* and other literary journals and publications. His short story collection, *The Way They Thought That Love Should Be,* included "The Glittering Kingdom," which was nominated for the Pushcart Prize. His first volume of poems, *Awake to Every Grace,* was published by Kelsay Press.

Roth recently completed his first novel, *As on a Darkling Plain.*

www.ingramcontent.com/pod-product-compliance
Lightning Source LLC
Chambersburg PA
CBHW031203160426
43193CB00008B/482